PEGASUS ENCYCLOPEDIA LIBRARY

AF587967

Space

MOON

Edited by: Pallabi B. Tomar, Hitesh Iplani
Managing editor: Tapasi De
Designed by: Vijesh Chahal, Anil Kumar, Rohit Kumar
Illustrated by: Suman S. Roy, Tanoy Choudhury
Colouring done by: Vinay Kumar, Kiran Kumari & Pradeep Kumar

CONTENTS

Astonishing fact

The oldest known map of the moon, about 5,000 years old was found carved into a rock in a prehistoric tomb at Knowth, County Meath, in Ireland.

The silvery moon

Moon is Earth's only natural satellite. It is the brightest object in the night sky but gives off no light of its own. Instead, it reflects light from the sun. Like the Earth and the rest of the solar system, the moon is about 4.6 billion years old.

The moon is a roughly spherical, rocky body orbiting the Earth at an average distance of 385,000 km. It measures about 3,475 km across, a little over one-quarter of Earth's diameter. Earth and the moon are the closest in size of any known planet and its satellite.

The moon has no life of any kind. Compared to the Earth, it has changed little over billions of years. On the moon, the sky is black even during the day and the stars are always visible.

The footprints left by Apollo astronauts will last for centuries because there is no wind on the moon. The moon does not possess any atmosphere, so there is no weather as we are used to on Earth. As there is no atmosphere to trap heat, the temperatures on the moon are extreme, ranging from 100 degree Celsius at noon to -173 degree Celsius at night!

The moon is covered with rocks, boulders, craters and a layer of charcoal-coloured soil from 1.5 to 6 m deep. The soil consists of rock fragments, pulverized rock and tiny pieces of glass. Two types of rock are found on the moon— **basalt**, which is hardened lava and **breccia**, which is soil and rock fragments that have melted together.

Astonishing fact

When Neil Armstrong took that historical step of 'one small step for man one giant step for mankind', it would not have occurred to anyone that the step he took in the dust of the moon was there to stay. It will be there for at least 10 million years!

The moon has no weather, no wind, rain or air. As a result, it has no protection from the sun's rays or meteorites and no ability to retain heat.

Origin and evolution of the moon

Scientists believe that the moon formed as a result of a collision known as the Giant Impact or the 'Big Whack.' According to this idea, Earth collided with a planet-sized object 4.6 billion years ago. As a result of the impact, a cloud of vaporized rock shot off Earth's surface and went into orbit around Earth. The cloud cooled and condensed into a ring of small, solid bodies, which then gathered together, forming the moon.

The rapid joining together of the small bodies released much energy as heat. Consequently, the moon melted, creating an 'ocean' of magma (melted rock).

The magma ocean slowly cooled and solidified. As it cooled, dense, iron-rich materials sank deep into the moon. Those materials also cooled and solidified, forming the mantle, the layer of rock beneath the crust.

Astonishing fact

Apollo 11 had only 20 seconds of fuel left when they landed on the moon!

The evolution of the moon has been completely different from that of the Earth. For about the first 700 million years of the moon's existence, it was struck by great numbers of meteorites. They blasted out craters of all sizes. The sheer impact of so many meteorites caused the moon's crust to melt. Eventually, as the crust cooled, lava from the interior surfaced and filled in cracks and some crater basins. These filled-in basins are the dark spots we see when we look at the moon.

To early astronomers, these dark regions appeared to be bodies of liquid. In 1609, the Italian astronomer Galileo Galilei became the first person to observe the moon through a telescope. He named these dark patches 'maria,' Latin for 'seas.'

In 1645, the Polish astronomer Johannes Hevelius, known as the father of lunar topography, charted 250 craters and other formations on the moon. Many of these were later named for philosophers and scientists, such as Danish astronomer Tycho Brahe, Polish astronomer Nicolaus Copernicus, German astronomer Johannes Kepler and Greek philosopher Plato.

Astonishing fact

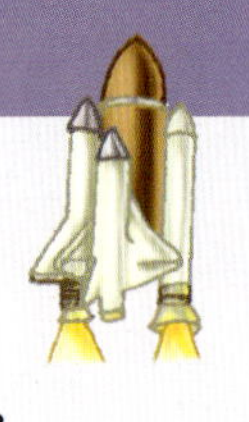

In China, the dark shadows that are on the moon are called 'the toad in the moon'.

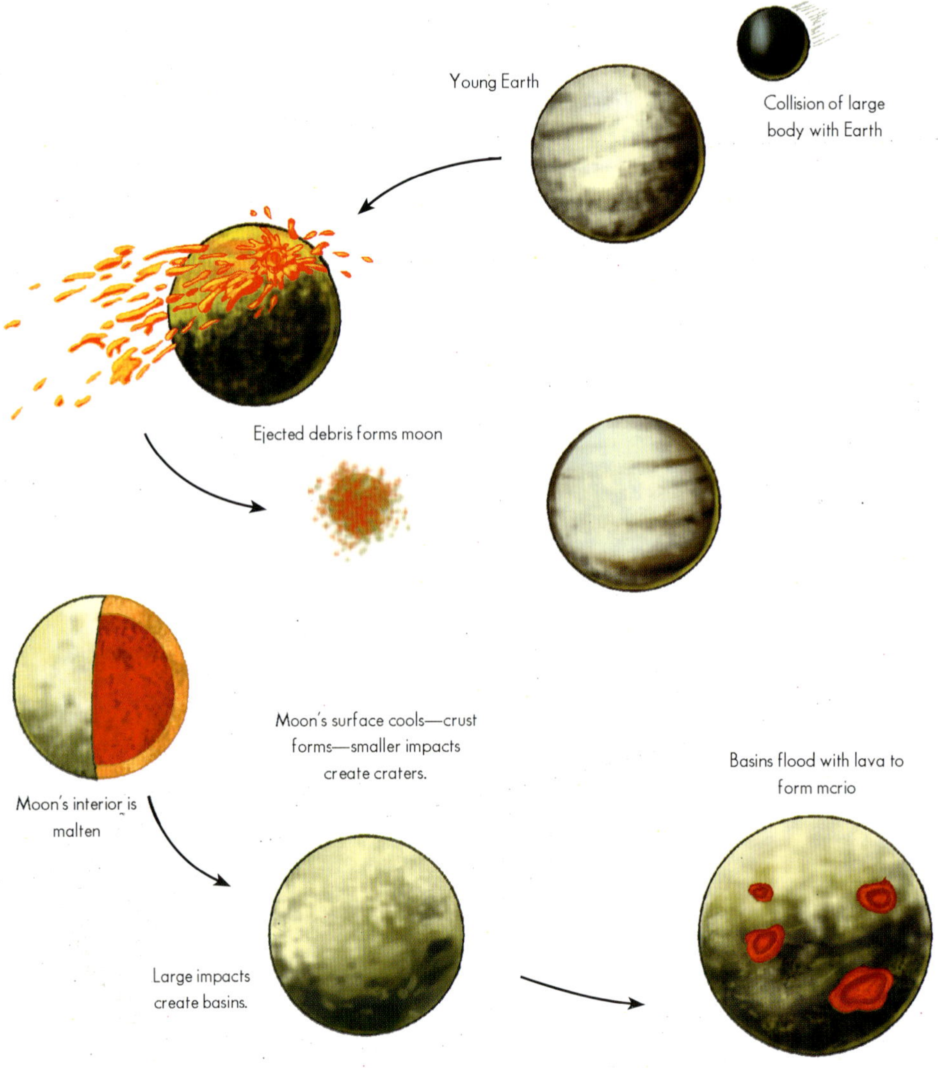

Birth of moon

Astonishing fact

The dark spots we see on the moon that create the image of the man in the moon are actually craters filled with basalt, which is a very dense material.

Composition of the moon

The moon's composition has been of great interest to scientists. With the collection of moon soil and moon rocks by astronauts, many questions have been answered. Moon soil contains no fossils of plants or animals, but when this soil is placed on Earth plants, they seem to grow better.

Moon rocks are composed of minerals including aluminum, calcium, magnesium, oxygen, silicon and titanium. Some gases are also trapped in these rocks, such as hydrogen and helium.

Astronauts collect two main types of rock, basalt and breccia. Basalt is formed from hardened lava and is made of feldspar, proxene and ilmenite crystals. These minerals were formed at 2200 degrees, which proves that the moon was extremely hot when it was forming. Breccia is made of soil and rock that have been squeezed together when hit by falling objects.

The interior of the moon

The moon, like the Earth, has three interior zones— crust, mantle and core. However, the composition, structure, and origin of the zones on the moon are much different from those on Earth.

Most of what scientists know about the interior of the moon has been learnt by studying moonquakes. The data on moonquakes come from scientific equipment set up by Apollo astronauts from 1969 to 1972.

Crust

The average thickness of the lunar crust is about 70 km, compared with about 10 km for Earth's crust. The outermost part of the moon's crust is broken, fractured and jumbled as a result of the large impacts it has endured. This shattered zone gives way to intact material below a depth of about 9 km. The bottom of the crust has an abrupt increase in rock density at a depth of about 60 km on the near side and about 80 km on the far side.

The moon's crust is composed of a dusty outer rock layer called a **regolith**. The term regolith refers to a rocky layer resembling concrete, which has been broken and blasted apart, then fused back together somehow. Like the Earth's crust, the moon's crust seems to contain some magnetism. Both the crust and regolith of the moon are unevenly distributed over the entire moon.

It takes about 1.25 seconds for moonlight to reach the Earth.

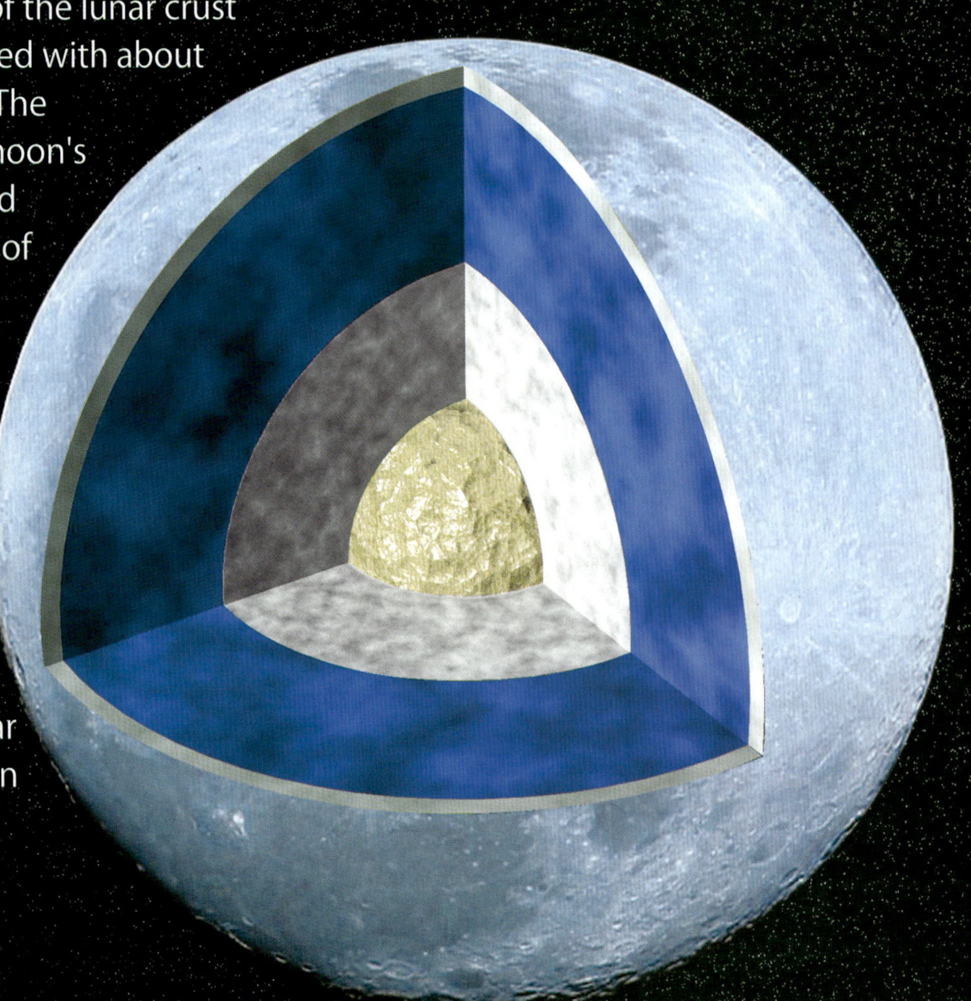

Mantle

The mantle of the moon consists of dense rocks that are rich in iron and magnesium. The mantle is formed during the period of global melting. Low-density minerals floated to the outer layers of the moon, while dense minerals sank deeper into it.

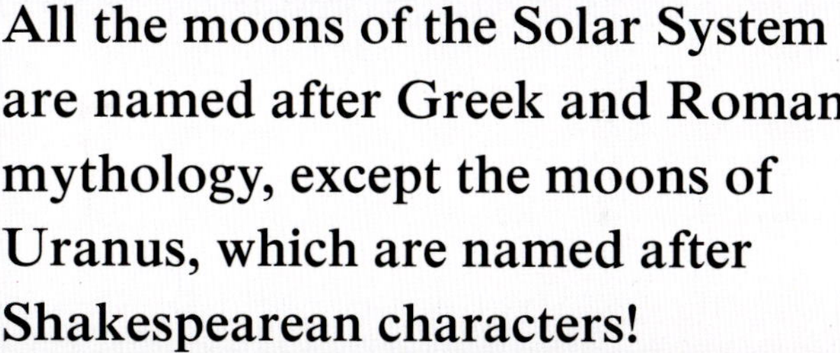

Astonishing fact

All the moons of the Solar System are named after Greek and Roman mythology, except the moons of Uranus, which are named after Shakespearean characters!

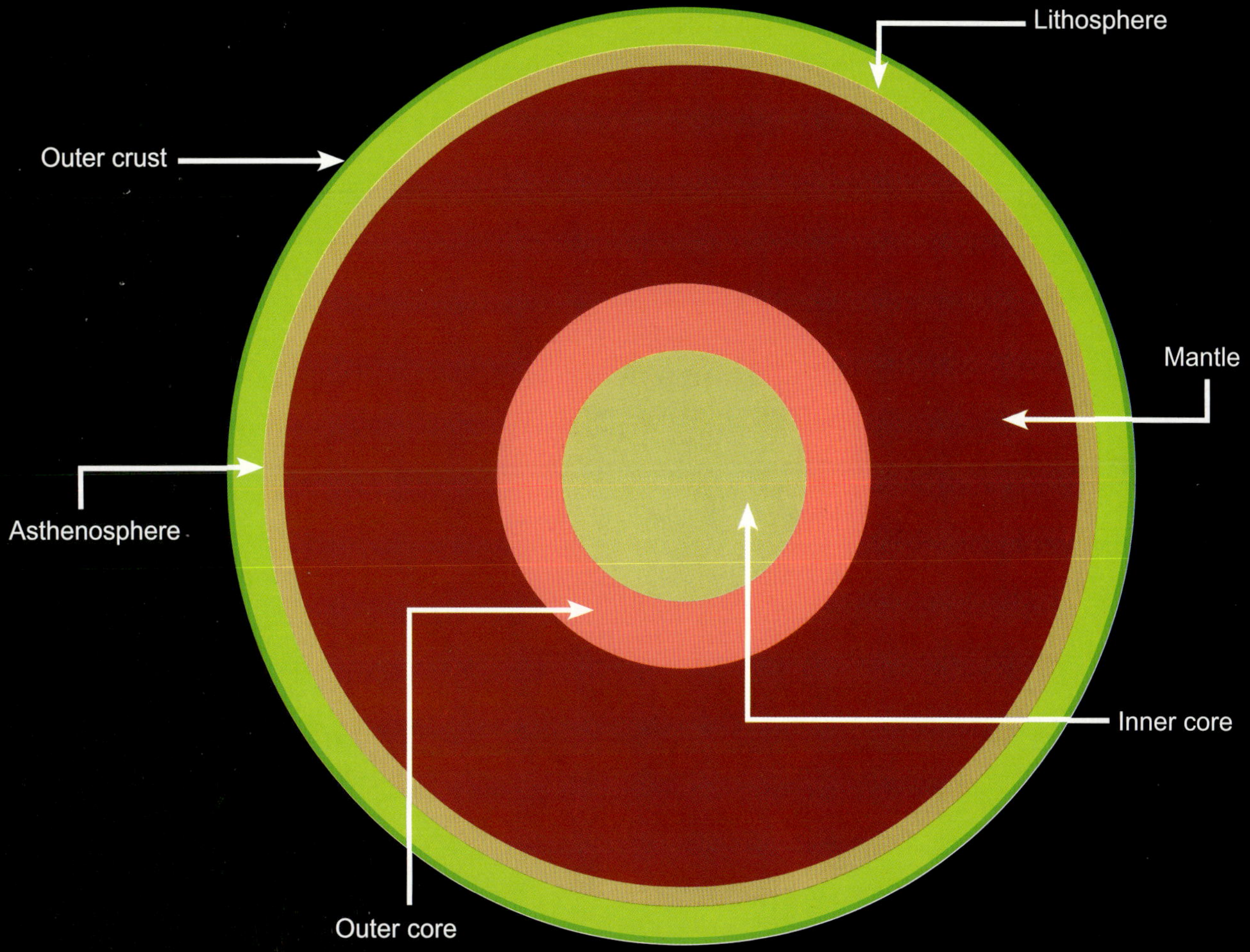

Later, the mantle partly melted due to heat building up in the deep interior. The source of the heat was probably the decay (breakup) of uranium and other radioactive elements. This melting produced basaltic magmas—bodies of molten rock. The magmas later made their way to the surface and erupted as mare lavas and ashes. Although, mare volcanism occurred for more than 1 billion years, much less than 1 per cent of the volume of the mantle ever remelted.

Lithosphere

Outer crust

Mantle

Asthenosphere

Inner core

Outer core

Core

The core has a radius of only about 400 km. By contrast, the radius of Earth's core is about 3,500 km.

The lunar core has less than 1 per cent of the mass of the moon. Scientists suspect that the core consists mostly of iron, and it may also contain large amounts of sulphur and other elements.

Earth's core is made mostly of molten iron and nickel. This rapidly rotating molten core is responsible for Earth's magnetic field. A magnetic field is an influence that a magnetic object creates in the region around it. If the core of a planet or a satellite is molten, motion within the core caused by the rotation of the planet or satellite makes the core magnetic. But the small, partly molten core of the moon cannot generate a magnetic field for the entire moon. However, small regions on the lunar surface are magnetic. Scientists are not sure how these regions acquired magnetism. Perhaps the moon once had a larger, more molten core.

There is evidence that the interior of the moon formerly contained gas, and that some gas may still be there. Basalt from the moon contains holes called vesicles that are created during a volcanic eruption.

Astonishing fact 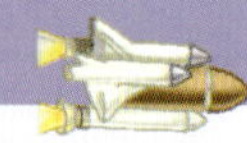

When the moon is directly over our head, we weigh slightly less!

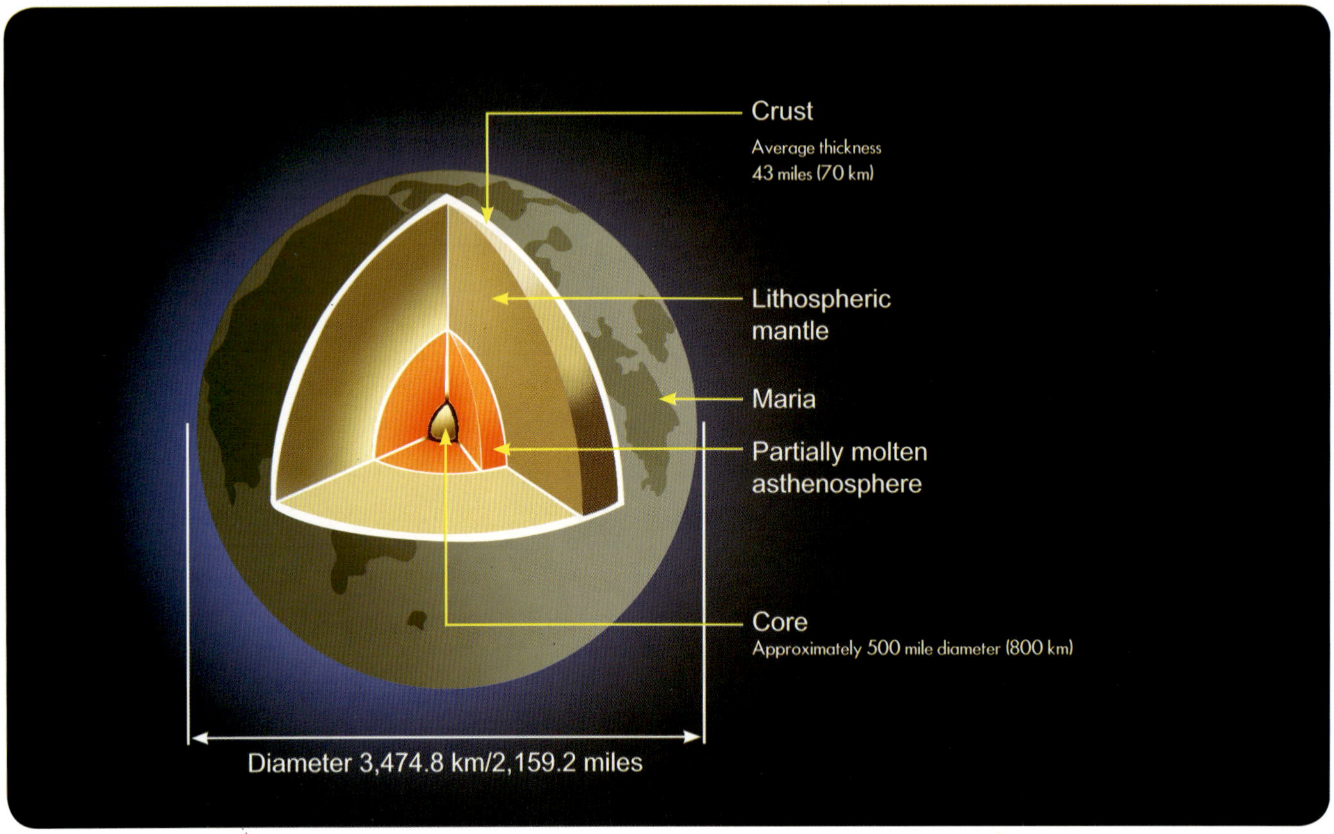

Crust
Average thickness
43 miles (70 km)
Lithospheric mantle
Maria
Partially molten asthenosphere
Core
Approximately 500 mile diameter (800 km)
Diameter 3,474.8 km/2,159.2 miles

Physical characteristics

Distance

The moon is approximately 384,400 km from the Earth. A radio signal from the Earth and bounced off the moon's surface back to Earth would take approximately 2 seconds. Communication with an astronaut on the moon would thus have several seconds pause between a question and an answer.

Mass

The moon's mass is 7.35 x 10 22 kg, about 1/81 of the Earth's mass.

Density

The density of the moon is 3340 kg/m^3.

Temperature

The average temperature on the surface of the moon during the day is 107 degree Celsius. That is hot enough to boil water on the Earth. During the night, the average temperature drops to −153 degree Celsius.

Atmosphere

The moon has no atmosphere. On the moon, the sky always appears dark. Also, since sound waves travel through air, there can be no sound transmission on the moon.

The moon weighs 81 billion tons.

Size

The moon's diameter is 3,476 km, 27 per cent of the diameter of the Earth. The gravitational tidal influence of the moon on the Earth is about twice as strong as the sun's gravitational tidal influence. The Earth: moon size ratio is quite small in comparison to ratios of most other planet: moon systems (for most planets in our solar system, the moons are much smaller in comparison to the planet and have less of an effect on the planet).

Gravity

Due to its smaller size and mass, the gravity of the moon is about 1/6 the gravity of the Earth. That means that a person who weighs 81 kg on Earth would only weigh 13 kg, if measured on the moon! That is why when the astronauts were on the moon, they were able to jump so high, even while wearing the heavy space suit.

The force of gravity from the moon affects the Earth. Its gravity reaches the Earth and pulls the oceans toward the moon, causing the tides. The gravity from the sun also affects the tides. The highest tides always occur when the moon and sun are aligned. That is when there is a New moon or a Full moon.

Astonishing fact

It wasn't until 1665 that scientists realized that other moons orbited other planets. Earth's moon's official name then became a capitalized 'Moon'.

Mare

Mare (plural maria) means 'sea,' but maria on the moon are plains on the moon. They are called maria because earlier astronomers thought that these areas on the moon were great seas. The first moon landing was in the Mare Tranquillitatis (the Sea of Tranquility). Maria is concentrated on the side of the moon that faces the Earth.

Maria are lowland rocks that are covered with a thin layer of rocky soil. The light spots are parts on the moon where it is mountainous, called the highlands. Most of the maria were formed about 3.3 to 3.8 billion years ago by lava flows.

Craters and Rilles

The surface of the moon is scarred by millions of (mostly circular) impact craters caused by asteroids, comets and meteorites. There is no atmosphere on the moon to help protect it from bombardment. Also, there is no erosion and little geologic activity to wear away these craters, so they remain unchanged until another new impact changes it.

A rille is a long, narrow valley on the surface of the moon. Hadley Rille is 125 km long, 400 m deep and almost 1500 m wide at its widest point.

Rille

Astonishing fact

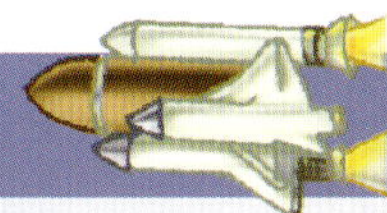

Some of the moon's craters originated internally, yet there is no indication that the moon was ever so hot enough to produce volcanic eruptions.

Jupiter's moon Ganymede is the largest moon in the Solar System and is larger than the planets Mercury and Pluto.

Libration

Libration is a rocking movement of the moon. Librations cause us to see the moon from different angles at different times, enabling us to see about 59 per cent of the moon's surface from Earth, even though the same side always faces us.

Shape of the moon

One important and beautiful phenomenon about the shape of the moon as it appears to the Earth is its 'waxing and waning'. The orbiting of the moon around the Earth and its own axis and the Earth's rotation around its axis causes this occurrence. Actually, no waxing and waning take place.

It is the illuminated portion of the moon that appears to the Earth make the people think so. The illuminated portion of the moon varies daily with the movement of the Earth, moon and the sun.

Mountains on the moon

There are several mountains and mountain ranges on the moon. Some of them are well over 3048 m tall. Most of the mountains on the moon are on the rims of large craters formed by meteorite impacts. The moon does not have jagged mountains; instead the moon's mountains are round and smooth.

Astonishing fact

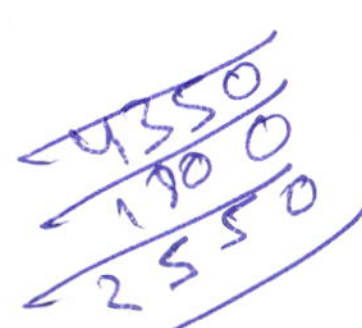

Moonquakes, which originate several miles below the moon's surface, maybe a result of the Earth's gravitational pull.

Magnetic field

Compared to that of Earth, the moon has a very weak magnetic field. While some of the moon's magnetism is thought to be intrinsic, collision with other celestial bodies might have bestowed some of the moon's magnetic properties. Indeed, a long-standing question in planetary science is whether an airless solar system body, such as the moon, can obtain magnetism by the impact processes from comets and asteroids. Magnetic measurements can also supply information about the size and electrical conductivity of the lunar core — evidence that will help scientists better understand the moon's origins.

Orbit

The moon moves in a variety of ways. For example, it rotates on its axis, an imaginary line that connects its poles. The moon also orbits the Earth. Different amounts of the moon's lighted side become visible in phases because of the moon's orbit around Earth. During events called eclipses, the moon is positioned in line with Earth and the sun.

The Earth's moon is the fifth largest in the whole solar system, and is bigger than the planet Pluto. The moon has a nearly circular orbit which is tilted about 5 degree towards the plane of the Earth's orbit. Its average distance from the Earth is 384,400 km. The combination of the moon's size and its distance from the Earth causes the moon to appear the same size in the sky as the sun, which is one reason we can have total solar eclipses.

Astonishing fact

The moon's gravity has slowed the speed of Earth's rotation. Long ago, it was much faster and days were much shorter.

It takes the moon 27.322 days to go around the Earth once. Due to this motion, the moon appears to move about 13 degree against the stars each day, or about one-half degree per hour. If you watch the moon over the course of several hours one night, you will notice that its position among the stars will change by a few degrees. The changing position of the moon with respect to the sun leads to lunar phases.

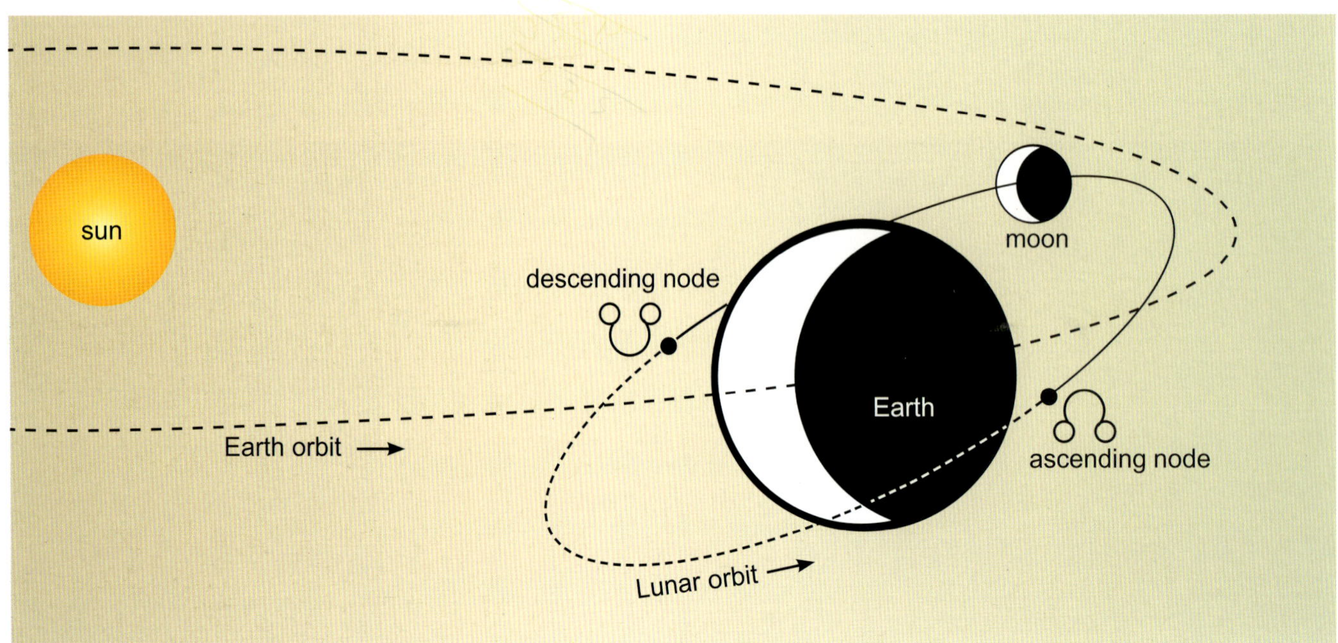

It takes the moon the same amount of time to rotate around once as it does for the moon to go around the Earth once. Therefore, Earth-bound observers can never see the 'far-side' of the moon. Tidal forces cause many of the moons of our solar system to have this type of orbit.

The moon's orbit is expanding over time. For example, a billion years ago, the moon was much closer to the Earth (roughly 200,000 km) and took only 20 days to orbit the Earth. Also, one Earth day was about 18 hours long (instead of our 24 hour day). The tides on Earth were also much stronger since the moon was closer to the Earth.

Saros

The saros is the roughly 18-year periodic cycle of the Earth-moon-sun system. Every 6,585 days, the Earth, moon and sun are in exactly the same position. When there is a lunar eclipse, there will also be one exactly 6,585 days later.

Approximately 49 moons can fit into our Earth.

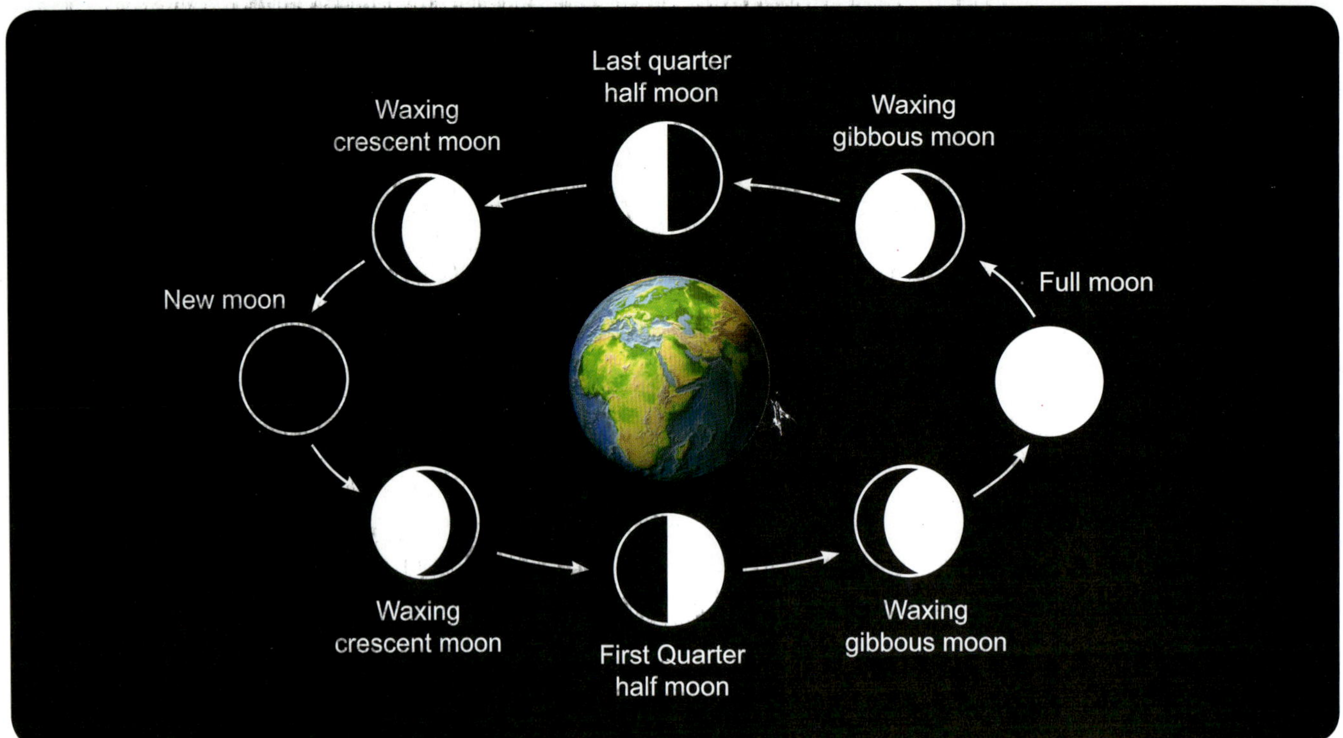

As the moon orbits the Earth, an observer on Earth can see the moon appear to change shape. It seems to change from a crescent to a circle and back again. The shape looks different from one day to the next because the observer sees different parts of the moon's sunlit surface as the moon orbits Earth. The different appearances are known as the **phases of the moon**.

The moon has four phases— new moon, first quarter, full moon and last quarter. When the moon is between the sun and Earth, its sunlit side is turned away from Earth. Astronomers call this darkened phase a new moon.

The next night after a new moon, a thin crescent of light appears along the moon's eastern edge. The remaining portion of the moon that faces Earth is faintly visible because of sunlight reflected from Earth to the moon. Each night, an observer on the Earth can see more of the sunlit side as the line between sunlight and dark, moves westward. After about seven days, the observer can see half a full moon, commonly called a half moon. This phase is known as the **first quarter**. About seven days later, the moon is on the side of Earth opposite the sun. The entire sunlit side of the moon is now visible. This phase is called a **full moon**.

Astonishing fact

The moon is 400 times smaller than the sun, but it is also 400 times closer to Earth. So from Earth, the moon and the sun look about the same size.

About seven days after a full moon, the observer again sees a half moon. This phase is the last quarter or third quarter. After another seven days, the moon is between Earth and the sun, and another new moon occurs.

As the moon changes from new moon to full moon, and more and more of it becomes visible, it is said to be **waxing**. As it changes from full moon to new moon, and less and less of it can be seen, it is **waning**. When the moon appears smaller than a half moon, it is called **crescent**. When it looks larger than a half moon, but is not yet a full moon, it is called **gibbous**.

Like the sun, the moon rises in the east and sets in the west. As the moon progresses through its phases, it rises and sets at different times. In the new moon phase, it rises with the sun and travels close to the sun across the sky.

The entire surface of the moon is covered in a layer of crushed and powdered rocks called the regolith. The dust is a result of millions of years of bombardment from space by tiny micrometeorites.

Eclipses occur when Earth, the sun and the moon are in a straight line or nearly so. A **lunar eclipse** occurs when the Earth gets directly or almost directly between the sun and the moon, and Earth's shadow falls on the moon. A lunar eclipse can occur only during a full moon. A solar eclipse occurs when the moon gets directly or almost directly between the sun and Earth, and the moon's shadow falls on Earth. A **solar eclipse** can occur only during a new moon.

During one part of each lunar orbit, the Earth is between the sun and the moon and during another part of the orbit; the moon is between the sun and Earth. But in most cases, the astronomical bodies are not aligned directly enough to cause an eclipse. Instead, Earth casts its shadow into space above or below the moon, or the moon casts its shadow into space above or below Earth.

Astonishing fact

An annular eclipse occurs when the moon is too small to block the whole sun and leaves a ring of light visible. This eclipse happens because the moon's orbit is not a perfect circle, so when the moon is farthest away from Earth, it appears smaller in the sky.

As the moon circles the Earth, the shape of the moon appears to change. This is because different amounts of the illuminated part of the moon are facing us. The shape varies from a full moon (when the Earth is between the sun and the moon) to a new moon (when the moon is between the sun and the Earth).

Blue moon

When two full moons occur in a single month, the second full moon is called a '**Blue** moon.' Another definition of the blue moon is the third full moon that occurs in a season of the year which has four full moons (usually each season has only three full moons).

Crescent moon

A crescent moon is part way between a half moon and a new moon or between a new moon and a half moon.

Full moon

A full moon appears as an entire circle in the sky. The full moon is given different names, depending on when it appears. For example, the 'Harvest moon' is the full moon that appears nearest to the Autumnal Equinox, occurring in late September or early October.

Astonishing fact

A full day on the moon, from one sunrise to the next, lasts about 29 Earth days on average.

Gibbous moon

A gibbous moon is between a full moon and a half moon.

Half moon

A half moon looks like half a circle. It is sometimes called a quarter moon. This moon has completed one quarter of an orbit around the Earth from either the full or new position and one quarter of the moon's surface is visible from the Earth.

New moon

The new moon is the phase of the moon when the moon is not visible from the Earth, because the side of the moon that is facing us is not being lit by the sun.

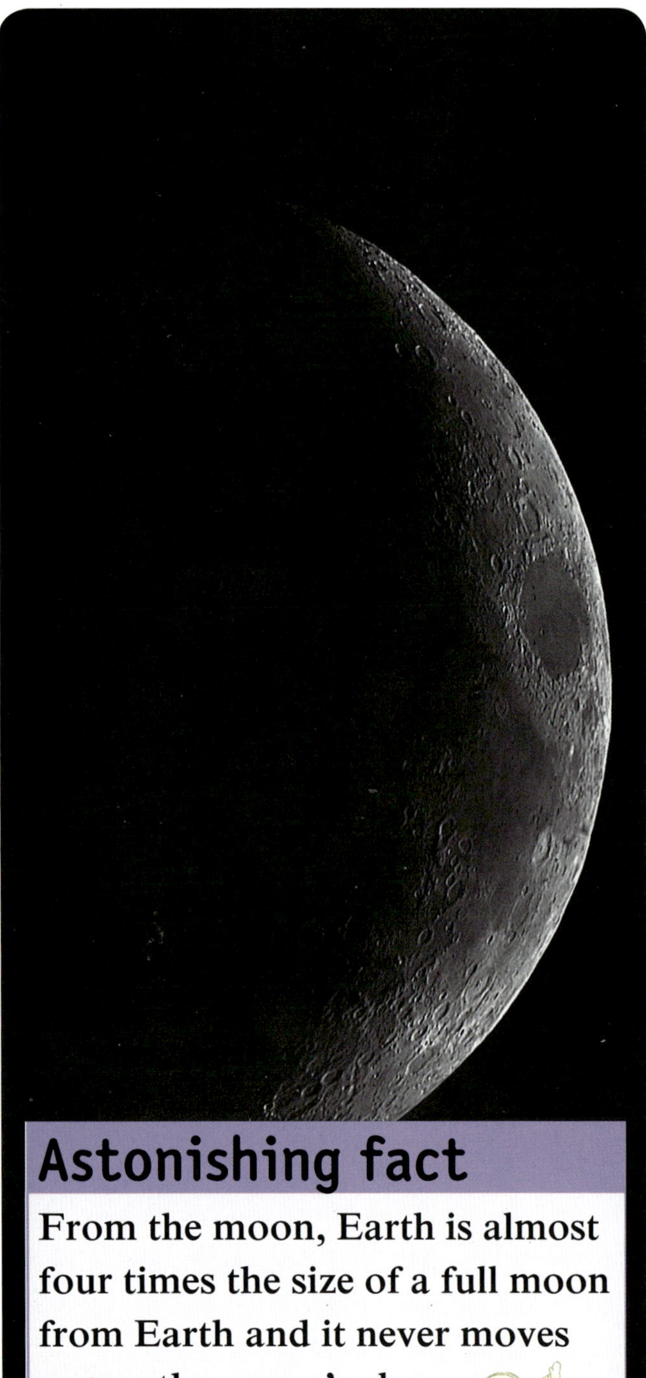

Astonishing fact

From the moon, Earth is almost four times the size of a full moon from Earth and it never moves across the moon's sky.

Relation with the Earth

The moon and the Earth are held together by gravity. The Earth is much more massive than the moon causing the moon to orbit the Earth. The moon revolves eastwards (counter clockwise). Each orbit takes 27.3 days. The moon also rotates or spins on an internal axis once every 27.3 days. The rotation and revolution of the moon is the same generally due to gravitational attraction of the moon to the Earth. It makes one rotation per revolution.

The moon's orbit around the Earth is slightly elliptical or oval-shaped. At its closest point called **perigee**, the moon is 363,000 km from the Earth. At its maximum distance called **apogee**, the moon is 405,000 km away. Apogee and perigee are highly elliptical.

Astonishing fact

As there is no atmosphere on the moon, there is no twilight before nightfall.

There are at least three reasons why the orbits of the moon and Earth are elliptical. First, due to their rotation, both bodies are slightly wider at the equator than between the poles. They are not perfect spheres, which makes their orbits a little erratic. Second, it is also possible that moon's internal structure is slightly uneven, which would also contribute to an elliptical orbit.

The gravitational forces between the Earth and the moon cause some interesting effects. The most obvious is the tides. The moon's gravitational attraction is stronger on the side of the Earth nearest to the moon and weaker on the opposite side. The gravitational pull of the moon tugs on the surface of the ocean until its water surface mounds up and outward in the direction of the moon. When the mound of water has reached its highest point it is called **high tide**. On the opposite side of the Earth from the moon, the centrifugal force caused by the Earth's rotation produces another mound of water and high tide. Between these two high tides are two flat areas on the surface of the ocean which are the low tides.

Each day there are two high tides and two low tides. The time between high and low tide is a little over 6 hours and the entire tidal cycle repeats itself four times each day. The regularity of the tides corresponds to the regular orbit of the moon around the Earth and the rotation of the Earth as it orbits around the sun.

Astonishing fact

The first person to draw a map of the moon as it appears through a telescope was British astronomer Thomas Harriot (c. 1560-1621).

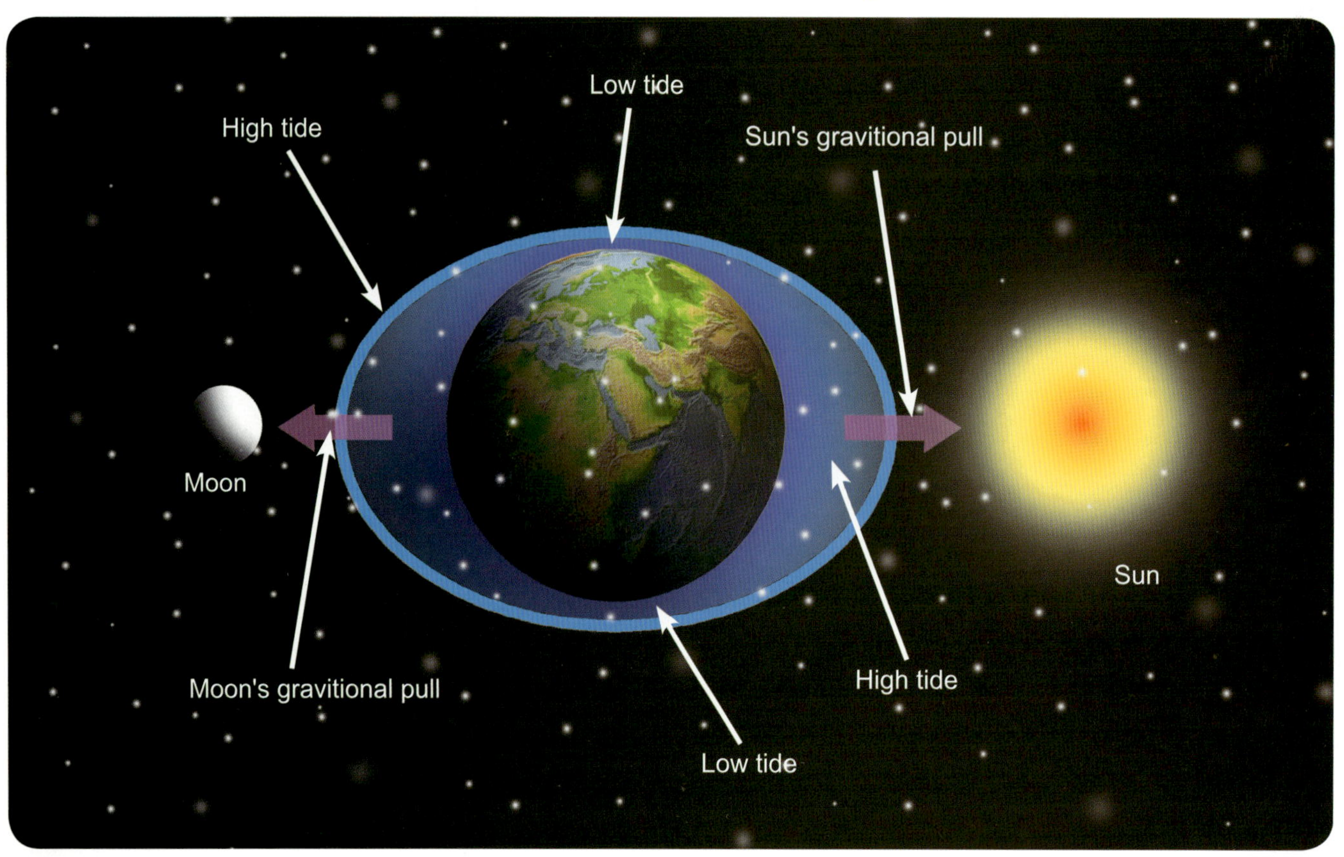

Study and exploration

Some Greek philosophers believed that the moon was a world much like Earth. In about A.D. 100, Plutarch even suggested that people lived on the moon. The Greeks also apparently believed that the dark areas of the moon were seas, while the bright regions were land.

In about A.D. 150, Ptolemy, a Greek astronomer said that the moon was Earth's nearest neighbour in space. He thought that both the moon and the sun orbited Earth. Ptolemy's views survived for more than 1,300 years. But by the early 1500's, the Polish astronomer Nicolaus Copernicus had developed the correct view—Earth and the other planets revolve around the sun and the moon orbits the Earth.

Astonishing fact

The Earth is 81 times heavier than the moon.

Apollo missions

Beginning in 1959, the Soviet Union and the United States sent a series of robot spacecraft to examine the moon in detail. Their ultimate goal was to land people safely on the moon. The United States finally reached that goal in 1969 with the landing of the Apollo 11 lunar module. The United States conducted six more Apollo missions, including five landings. The last of those was Apollo 17, in December 1972.

The Apollo missions revolutionized the understanding of the moon. Much of the knowledge gained about the moon also applies to Earth and the other inner planets like Mercury, Venus, and Mars. After the Apollo missions, the Soviets sent four Luna robot craft to the moon. The last, Luna 24, returned samples of lunar soil to Earth in August 1976.

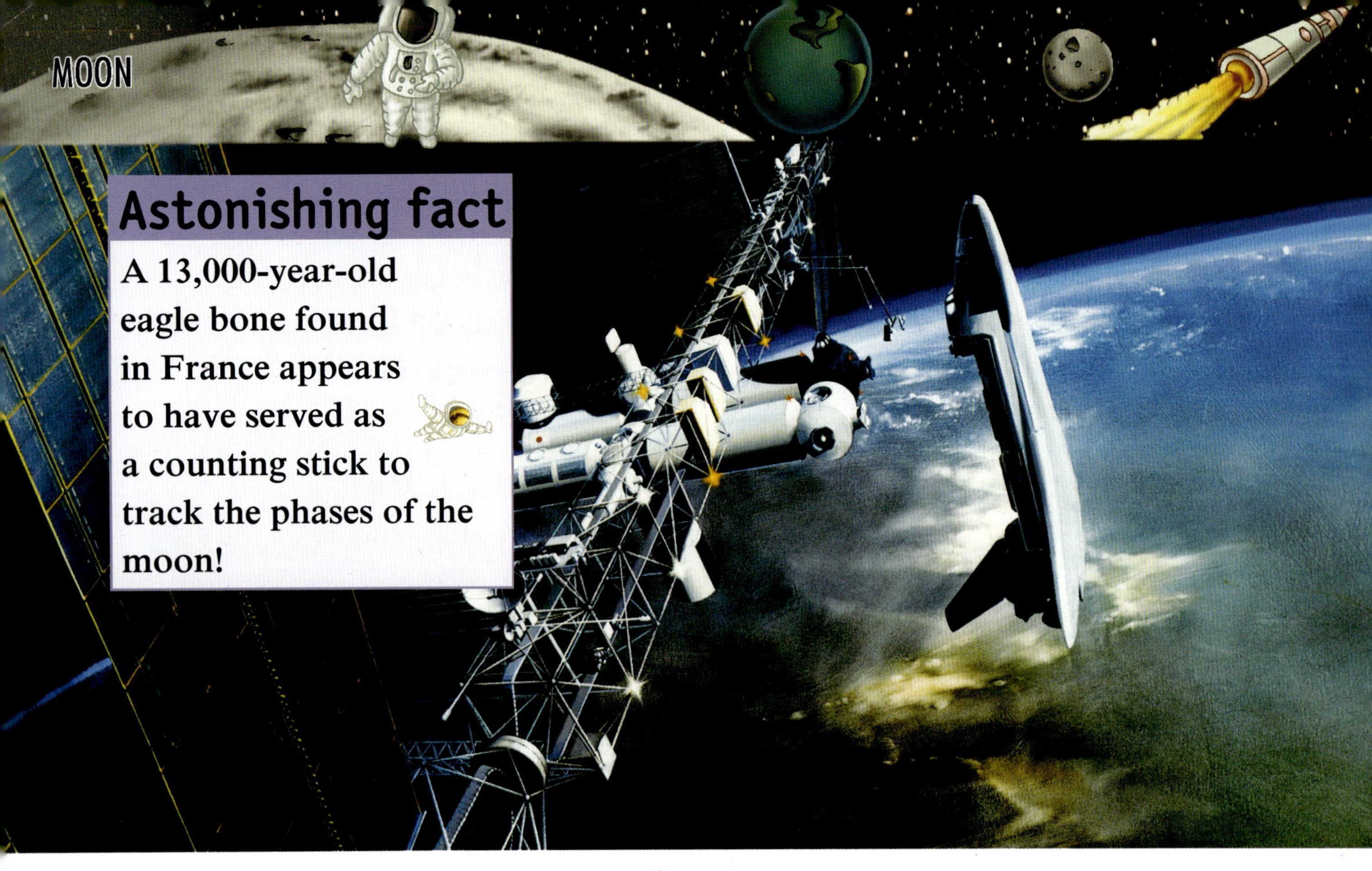

Astonishing fact

A 13,000-year-old eagle bone found in France appears to have served as a counting stick to track the phases of the moon!

In January 1959, a small Soviet sphere bristling with antennas, dubbed **Luna 1**, flew by the moon at a distance of some 5,995 km. Though Luna 1 did not impact the moon's surface, as was likely intended, its suite of scientific equipment revealed for the first time that the moon had no magnetic field. The craft also returned evidence of space phenomena, such as the steady flow of ionized plasma now known as solar wind.

First Landing

Later in 1959 **Luna 2** became the first spacecraft to land on the moon's surface when it impacted near the Aristides, Archimedes, and Autolycus craters. A third Luna mission subsequently captured the first, blurry, images of the far side of the moon.

In 1962 NASA placed its first spacecraft on the moon—**Ranger 4**. The Ranger missions were kamikaze missions (suicidal missions); the spacecraft were engineered to streak straight towards the moon and capture as many images as possible before crashing onto its surface. Unfortunately Ranger 4 was unable to return any scientific data before slamming into the far side of the moon.

Two years later, however, **Ranger 7** streaked toward the moon with cameras blazing and captured more than 4,000 photos in the 17 minutes before it smashed onto the surface. Images from all the Ranger missions, particularly **Ranger 9**, showed that the moon's surface was rough. They spotlighted the challenges of finding a smooth landing site on its surface.

In 1966 the Soviet spacecraft **Luna 9** overcame the moon's topographic hurdles and became the first vehicle to soft-land safely on the surface. The small craft was stocked with scientific and communications equipment and it photographed a ground level lunar panorama. **Luna 10** launched later that year became the first spacecraft to successfully orbit the moon.

The **Surveyor** space probes (1966-68) were the first Nasa craft to perform controlled landings on the moon's surface. Surveyor carried cameras to explore the moon's surface terrain, as well as soil samplers that analyzed the nature of lunar rock and dirt.

In 1966 and 1967 Nasa launched **lunar orbiters** that were designed to circle the moon and chart its surface in preparation for future manned landings. In total, five lunar orbiter missions photographed about 99 per cent of the moon's surface.

Man on the moon

These robotic probes paved the way for a giant leap forward in space exploration. On July 20, 1969, **Neil Armstrong** and **Edwin 'Buzz' Aldrin** became the first people to reach the moon when their **Apollo 11** lunar lander touched down in the Sea of Tranquility.

Astonishing fact

Aristotle and Pliny the Elder, the well-known Roman naturalist and author believed that a full moon affected the water in a human's brain, causing insanity or irrational behaviour.

Later missions carried a lunar rover that was driven across the satellite's surface, and saw astronauts spend as long as three days on the moon! Before the Apollo project ended in 1972, five other missions and a dozen men had visited the moon.

Astonishing fact

On November 17, 1970, the Soviet robot Lunokhod 1 (meaning 'the moon walker' in Russian) was the first vehicle to travel on the moon.

In 1994, Nasa again focused on the moon. The **Clementine** mission succeeded in mapping the moon's surface in wavelengths other than visible light, from ultraviolet to infrared.

Today India, China, and Japan all have lunar exploration projects in development. The United States own plan is perhaps the most ambitious—to return humans to the moon by 2020 and eventually use the moon as a staging point for human flight to Mars and beyond.

Moon in mythology

The moon has figured in human mythologies, often as a counterpart of the sun. In ancient times, it was not uncommon for cultures to believe that the moon died each night, thus descending into the underworld; other cultures believed that the moon chased the sun (and vice-versa).

The moon has figured prominently in various mythologies and folk beliefs. The numerous lunar deities are often female such as the Greek goddesses Selene and Artemis, their Roman equivalents Luna and Diana or the Thracian Bendis. However, males are also found, such as Nanna or Sin of the Mesopotamians, Thoth of the Egyptians and the Japanese god Susanowo and Tecciztecatl of the Aztecs.

The moon has a long association with insanity and irrationality. The words lunacy and loony are derived from the Latin name for the moon, Luna. Folklore also stated that shape shifters such as werewolves and weretigers, mythical creatures capable of changing form between human and beast, drew their power from the moon and would change into their bestial form during the full moon.

Di you know that the phrase 'once in a blue moon' traditionally refers to an impossible event or an event that rarely happens.

Many cultures around the world have interesting myths about the moon, reflecting its prominence in the night sky and its impact on our lives.

For thousands of years, humankind has charted life and living by the cycles of the moon. Farmers have planned their planting and harvesting cycles around the moon cycles. Hunters have hunted by the moon's phases, and fishermen in certain cultures have found that their biggest catch happens at the full moon. Priests and priestesses have planned ceremonies to coincide with the full or new moon.

It has also been found that in cultures which honour the cycles of the moon, women are held in a much higher regard than those women in cultures who do not honour the moon phases. Many ancient calendars were actually lunar based; so they had thirteen months, and to this day, several holidays are still dated according to the moon's phase (Easter, Passover and Ramadan).

Many ancient cultures named the full moons according to the time of year.

Astonishing fact

In astrology, the moon represents the inner nature of a person. The moon sign reveals a person's emotional and subconscious state. In Western astrology, the moon is associated to the maternal, while the sun is associated with fatherhood.

Test Your MEMORY

1. What is the moon?
2. Write briefly about how the moon was formed.
3. What is the moon composed of?
4. Write about the craters on the moon.
5. Describe two physical characteristics of the moon.
6. Write about the rotation and orbit of the moon.
7. Describe the phases of the moon.
8. Write in brief about the interior of the moon.
9. How is moon related to the Earth?
10. Write briefly about the history of moon study.
11. Write about some important moon missions.
12. Write about the role of moon in mythology.

Index

RIVOLUZIONE VEDOVA

a cura di / edited by
GABRIELLA BELLI

M9

FONDAZIONE
EMILIO E ANNABIANCA
VEDOVA

M9

Presidente / President
ALFREDO BIANCHINI

Consiglieri / Board of Directors
FABRIZIO GAZZARRI
BRUNO GIAMPAOLI
MAURIZIO MILAN
PHILIP RYLANDS

Collegio sindacale / Board of Auditors
RICCARDO AVANZI
VITTORIO RACCAMARI
MICHELE STIZ

Direttore archivio e collezione / Archive and Collection Director
FABRIZIO GAZZARRI

Organizzazione generale e mostre / General Organization and Exhibits
ELENA OYELAMI BIANCHINI

Ricerca scientifica / Research
CLELIA CALDESI VALERI
SONIA OSETTA
MADDALENA PUGLIESE

Coordinamento editoriale e social media / Editorial Coordination and Social Media
CLELIA CALDESI VALERI

Supporto organizzativo mostre / Exhibits Organization Support
MADDALENA PUGLIESE

Archivio / Archive
SONIA OSETTA

Archivio digitale e informatica / Digital Archive and IT
BRUNO ZANON

Identità grafica / Visual Identity
TWINSTUDIO, Milano / Milan
ELENA PEDRAZZINI

Comunicazione e ufficio stampa / Communication and Press Office
STUDIO SYSTEMA, Venezia / Venice
ADRIANA VIANELLO
ANDREA DE MARCHI
LIVIA SARTORI DI BORGORICCO

Presidente / President
MICHELE BUGLIESI

Direttore Generale / General Director
GIOVANNI DELL'OLIVO

Consiglio di Amministrazione / Board of Governors
MICHELE BUGLIESI
Presidente / President
VINCENZO MARINESE
Vice Presidente / Vice President
GIORGIO BALDO
MARIACRISTINA GRIBAUDI
STEFANO MELONI

Consiglio Generale / General Council
MICHELE BUGLIESI
Presidente / President
ANGELO TABARO
Vice Presidente / Vice President
BENNO ALBRECHT
EMANUELA BASSETTI
CARLO BOFFI FARSETTI
AGAR BRUGIAVINI
MAURIZIO CARLIN
GABRIELE GIAMBRUNO
TIZIANA LIPPIELLO
PAOLA MARINI
GIANPIERO MENEGAZZO
PAOLO ROBERTO RISOTTI
STEFANO SCALETTARIS
MASSIMO ZANON

Collegio dei revisori / Audit Committee
CRISTIANO CERCHIAI
ANTONIA COPPOLA
ANDREA VALMARANA

Fondazione
M9 - Museo del '900
Presidente / President
MICHELE BUGLIESI

Direttore Scientifico / Scientific Director
LUCA MOLINARI

Consiglio di Amministrazione / Board of Governors
MICHELE BUGLIESI
Presidente / President
ALBERTO FERLENGA
PAOLA MARINI

Revisore unico / Sole Auditor
ANDREA VALMARANA

M9 District
Presidente / President
MICHELE BUGLIESI

Direttore / Director
ANTONIO RIGON

Consiglio di Amministrazione / Board of Governors
MICHELE BUGLIESI
Presidente / President
VINCENZO MARINESE
TOMMASO SANTINI

Revisore unico / Sole Auditor
ANDREA VALMARANA

Fondazione Emilio e Annabianca Vedova con / with Fondazione M9 ringraziano per i prestiti / thank for the loans
BERLINISCHE GALERIE - LANDESMUSEUM FÜR MODERNE KUNST, FOTOGRAFIE UND ARCHITEKTUR, Berlino / Berlin
FONDAZIONE CARIVERONA, Verona

RIVOLUZIONE VEDOVA
5 maggio / May - 26 novembre / November 2023
Venezia Mestre, M9 - Museo del '900

Mostra ideata e prodotta / Exhibition conceived and produced by
FONDAZIONE EMILIO E ANNABIANCA VEDOVA
FONDAZIONE M9

A cura di / Curated by
GABRIELLA BELLI

Coordinamento generale / General Coordination
GIORGIO BALDO - Fondazione di Venezia
ELENA OYELAMI BIANCHINI - Fondazione Emilio e Annabianca Vedova

Coordinamento esecutivo / Executive Coordination
LUCA MOLINARI - Fondazione M9
SILVIA PELLIZZERI - Fondazione M9

Consulenza / Consultant
FABRIZIO GAZZARRI
Fondazione Emilio e Annabianca Vedova

Ricerca scientifica / Research
Fondazione Emilio e Annabianca Vedova
CLELIA CALDESI VALERI
SONIA OSETTA
MADDALENA PUGLIESE

Fondazione M9
LIVIO KARRER
MICHELANGELA DI GIACOMO
GIUSEPPE SACCÀ

Progetto di allestimento / Installation Design
ALVISI KIRIMOTO, Roma / Rome
MASSIMO ALVISI
JUNKO KIRIMOTO
SILVIA RINALDUZZI

Video, progetto grafico e immagine coordinata / Video, Graphic Design and Visuals
TWIN STUDIO, Milano / Milan
ELENA PEDRAZZINI
TOMASO PESSINA
ELISABETTA BIANCHI
NINA LEO
GAIA MANFREDI
OLGA STOPAZZOLO
LINA ARDILA
CHIARA FERINI

Progetto multimediale / Multimedia Project
VITRUVIO VIRTUAL REALITY, Bologna
ALESSANDRO AGOSTINI
MAURIZIO AGOSTINI
UBALDO RIGHI
SIMONE SALOMONI

Progettazione eventi collaterali / Side Event Planning
STEFANO CECCHETTO

Allestimenti / Installation
OTT ART

Trasporti / Transport
APICE

Assicurazioni / Insurance
MAG BROKER DI ASSICURAZIONE - SPECIALTY FINE ART
KUHN&BÜLOW

Illuminazione / Lighting
iGUZZINI

Supervisione allestimenti / Installation Supervision
CLAUDIA BIOTTO - M9 District

Responsabile della sicurezza / Security
PRISMA, Noventa di Piave

Coordinamento editoriale / Editorial Coordination
CLELIA CALDESI VALERI

Archivio digitale / Digital Archivist
BRUNO ZANON - Fondazione Emilio e Annabianca Vedova

Traduzioni / Translations
JOHN FRANCIS PHILLMORE
SIMON TURNER

Comunicazione e ufficio stampa / Communication and Press Office
STUDIO SYSTEMA, Venezia / Venice
ADRIANA VIANELLO
ANDREA DE MARCHI
LIVIA SARTORI DI BORGORICCO

COMIN & PARTNERS, Roma / Rome
ELENA DI GIOVANNI
DAMIANO BELTOTTO
FAUSTO FIORIN
RACHELE MANNOCCHI
BIANCA MINNITI

SILVIA PELLIZZERI - Fondazione M9
PAOLA SARTORE - Fondazione di Venezia

Social media e gestione dei contenuti digitali / Social Media and Digital Content Management
TWIN STUDIO, Milano *per / for* Fondazione Emilio e Annabianca Vedova
MARTA PETTINAU - Fondazione M9
FRANCESCA CARMIGNOLA - Fondazione M9

Servizi educativi / Educational Services
SILVIA FABRIS - Fondazione M9

Coordinamento servizi museali e biglietteria / Coordination of Museum and Ticketing Services
FEDERICA ZIA - Fondazione M9

Amministrazione / Administration
FRANCESCO TORRESAN - Fondazione M9
MICHELE BORELLA - Fondazione M9

Marketing e raccolta fondi / Marketing and Fundraising
DANIELA PAVAN *per / for* Fondazione M9
DANIELA FONTANA *per / for* Fondazione di Venezia

Gestione spazi ed eventi / Location and Event Manager
SILVIA CARRARO - M9 District

Cerimoniale e segreteria / Ceremonial and Secretariat
FRANCESCA BORSATO - Fondazione M9
LAURA LAGHI - Fondazione di Venezia
GIORGIA ZANON - Fondazione di Venezia

Servizi museali, supporto tecnico e biglietteria / Maintenance, Museum and Ticketing Services
RNB4CULTURE, Milano

Con il patrocinio di / Under the Aegis of

Main sponsor

Sponsor

Official partner

Nei giorni di attesa della mostra *Rivoluzione Vedova* mi è stata rivolta, frequentemente, la domanda: perché mai l'esposizione a Mestre all'M9 - Museo del '900? Come mai in un luogo così diverso, lontano dal suggestivo, consueto e tradizionale veneziano Spazio Vedova al Magazzino del Sale, lungo quell'unica "strada liquida" che è il canale della Giudecca? Un luogo diverso e lontano, lontano da dove?

In realtà, come è ormai generalmente riconosciuto dagli studiosi e interpreti della personalità e dell'opera di Vedova, l'arte per Vedova non è mai stata un'attività, bensì un modo di esistere e di essere: aggiungerei che era il suo stesso incedere nel mondo. Il suo è stato un urlo di denuncia dei mali e delle ingiustizie umane: un urlo costante diretto a ignoti infiniti interlocutori e spettatori e verso ignoti infiniti mondi, per cui si può ben dire che per lui non vi siano mai stati luoghi vicini e lontani perché la sua centralità non dipendeva e non dipende, non era condizionata e non è condizionata, dalla fisicità di un luogo bensì dall'intensità e dalla forza del suo messaggio.

Certo è anche vero che le opere d'arte e gli spazi che le circondano vivono quasi simbioticamente in un rapporto di interdipendenza: d'altronde, secondo una ben nota teoria estrema postmoderna, quasi paradossale, l'installazione di qualsiasi oggetto in un determinato e particolare contesto sarebbe di per sé sufficiente a indurre una trasfigurazione dell'opera in un diverso oggetto artistico (o addirittura trasformare in artistico un oggetto che pur non avesse un'originaria connotazione riconducibile a un perimetro artistico).

Ebbene, M9 è uno spazio museale straordinario (ideato e progettato, come noto, nel centro di Mestre da Sauerbruch Hutton) nel cui ambito la superficie dedicata alla mostra di Vedova è un vero e proprio "territorio", all'ultimo piano, unico e continuo di circa 1350 metri quadrati, circondati da spazi collaterali che interagiscono con lo spazio centrale.

La mostra, la prima dedicata all'arte contemporanea da M9, è progettata e curata magistralmente da Gabriella Belli ed è "messa in scena" dagli autorevolissimi architetti Massimo Alvisi e Junko Kirimoto. La mostra propone, fra altro, i giganteschi *Absurdes Berliner Tagebuch '64*, *...in continuum, compenetrazioni/traslati '87/'88*, centodue dipinti in un'unica installazione senza soluzione di continuità e, ancora, i *Dischi*, lavori realizzati negli anni ottanta.

Sono opere, come ci ricorda Gabriella Belli, nate dalla struggente necessità di Vedova di dare voce a quel «malessere dentro questa società e volerne un'altra» (così diceva Vedova, appunto, nel cuore della protesta del 1968).

La qualità stessa delle opere esposte dimostra l'impegno profuso da Fondazione Vedova per onorare la proposta di M9. Ma è anche da aggiungere che la volontà di dare seguito all'invito di M9 è stata accompagnata da un altro pensiero: quello di offrire una testimonianza concreta di un legame fra Mestre e Venezia il

In these days of waiting for the new *Rivoluzione Vedova* exhibition to open I have frequently been asked: Why is the show at the M9 - Museo del '900 in Mestre? Why in such a different setting, far from the usual evocative, the traditional Venetian, Spazio Vedova at the Magazzino del Sale, beside that unique "liquid highway" that is the Giudecca Canal? A different and a far-off venue: but far from where?

In fact, as is nowadays generally acknowledged by scholars and interpreters of Vedova's life and work, art for Vedova was never an activity apart, but more a mode of existence: I could add that it was how he strode through the world. He was always ready to raise his voice in denunciation of human ills and injustices: a voice raised in anger and constantly directed at unknown infinite interlocutors and spectators, and towards unknown infinite worlds, so that we could well say that for him no place was nearer or further off because what was central to him did not depend and does not depend on, was not and is not conditioned by, the physical location of any place, but on the power and intensity of his message.

Of course, it is also true that works of art and the spaces that surround them live in an almost symbiotic, interdependent relationship. Furthermore, according to a well-known extreme, almost paradoxical post-modern theory, the placing of any object in any given, particular context is in itself sufficient to transfigure the work into a different art object (or even transform into art an object that might originally have lacked any artistic connotation).

M9 is an extraordinary museum space in the centre of Mestre (designed, as we know, by international architects Sauerbruch Hutton) in which the area on the top floor dedicated to the Vedova exhibition is a real "arena", a single continuous space of some 1350 square metres, surrounded by collateral secondary spaces that interact with the central hall.

The exhibition, incidentally the first M9 show to be dedicated to contemporary art, has been masterfully designed and curated by Gabriella Belli and mounted by the influential architects Massimo Alvisi and Junko Kirimoto. The exhibition offers, among other works, the gigantic *Absurdes Berliner Tagebuch '64*, *...in continuum, compenetrazioni/traslati '87/'88* — 102 paintings in a single seamless installation — and concludes with the celebrated *Dischi* from the 1980s. They are works, Gabriella Belli reminds us, born out of Vedova's aching need to give voice to the "distress at being within this society and desiring another" (as the artist himself put it in the heat of his involvement with the 1968 protest movements).

The very quality of the works on display is demonstration enough of the Fondazione Vedova's commitment to do honour to M9's proposition. But we should also add that our willingness to embrace the museum's invitation was accompanied by another thought: that of offering a concrete testimony of the link between Mestre and Venice whose destiny is now firmly a